The Secret of Wealth Creation

By Paapa Owusu-Manu

Published by New Generation Publishing in 2014

Copyright © Paapa Owusu-Manu 2014

First Edition

Unless otherwise indicated, all scripture quotations are taken from New Living Translation, New International Version, King James Version of the Bible
The author asserts the moral right under the Copyright, Designs and Patents Act 1988 to be identified as the author of this work.

All Rights reserved. No part of this publication may be reproduced, stored in a retrieval system or transmitted, in any form or by any means without the prior consent of the author, nor be otherwise circulated in any form of binding or cover other than that which it is published and without a similar condition being imposed on the subsequent purchaser.

www.newgeneration-publishing.com

 New Generation Publishing

Table of Contents

Introduction 6
The Secret of Wealth Creation:
The D Factor 10
Discomfort 10
Dream 12
Prayer – One 13
Discernment 14
Divine Direction 15
Prayer – Two 18
Discipline 20
Saving Plan 22
Determination 28
Prayer – Three 39
Diligence 42
Discovery 48
Development 48
Self and Business 49
Self-Development 49
Business development 50
Sources of Finance 51
Own Income or Savings 51
Family or Friends 51
Investors 54
Bank 55

Directorship 56
Examples of some
Bible entrepreneurs 56
Enterprise & Entrepreneurial Characteristics
.... 63
Prayer – Four 64
Entrepreneurship and Business
Idea Generation Exercise 66
Prayer – Five 71
Invitation to Jesus Christ 71
Other Publications 73

ACKNOWLEDGEMENT

I thank the Almighty God, God of Abraham, God of Isaac and God of Jacob, the Covenant-keeping God for calling me into His glorious Kingdom as one of His servants in this age. Father of mercies and grace, God the Son and God the Holy Spirit, your presence in my life has brought me this far with this book as a present to your children.

I also give special thanks to my spiritual father the Major Prophet Elisha K. Boateng (Founder and General Overseer, Mountain Movers Chapel International) and his wife Pastor Florence Opoku Boateng for their prayers, support, training and love towards my family.

I am greatly indebted to my lovely wife, Pastor Joyce Owusu-Manu for sticking by me in times of difficulties and financial hardships, not forgetting the support of my children Obaapa, Onuapa and Onyamenipa Daniel.

I am deeply grateful to all my work colleagues, my pastor friends, particularly all pastors of Mountain Movers Chapel International, my good friend Pastor Robert Ato Sakyi and Prophet James Kwaku Dellah-Gu (founder of Live Glory Ministries International), Ghana for their encouragement, kindness and support to my family.

A special thanks to my elder brother Dr. Abubakar Manu of University of Legon, Ghana.

I again extend a heartfelt thanks and gratitude to all the members of MMCI, London, especially the Bible Students of Elisha's School of Prophecy.

I express my sincere appreciation to the following people who spent their precious time by proofreading and offering constructive criticism and suggestions: Dr. Binanda Barkakaty and Senior Ministers Kwamena Arko and Esther Kigozi of MMCI London.

My final gratitude is to my mother, Susana Asama Manu and siblings for their prayers and encouragement.

DEDICATION

To my wife, Joyce and children (Obaapa, Onuapa and Onyamenipa Daniel).

THE SECRET OF WEALTH CREATION

BREAKING THE CYCLE OF POVERTY

Introduction

The Bible clearly states that money is a defence and money answers all things. Wisdom without money is considered foolishness and the Bible is also clear on this fact that without money, wisdom cannot be remembered. Every child of God should pray that God blesses him/her financially with no added sorrows. Poverty is a curse that places limitations on the lives of many people. Poverty is more severe than sickness and diseases, leading to the collapse of many marriages and creating problems in homes around the world. It brings humiliation, shame and disgrace. It makes people lie and ruins friendship and relationships.

If God does not show you mercy, poverty can cause you to miss heaven. With poverty some people live and others indulge in dirty means of exonerating themselves from the chains of poverty. Many people are suffering financially and struggle to come out of it. Some people do try all means and even engage in dubious means to come out of financial slavery. Some are able to come out of a financial mess but others are drowned in it forever. Some people are born into poverty and it becomes a problem they fight from generation to generation. Others also become poor through diverse means, i.e. mismanagement through lack of budgeting and financial planning, unnecessary borrowing or

THE SECRET OF WEALTH CREATION

BREAKING THE CYCLE OF POVERTY

mishandling of money. Some people become victims of financial slavery through sickness, loss of job, marriage problems, breakdown of families, or business failures.

Some Christians become poor and remain in poverty because of laziness, idleness, improper application of knowledge or misinterpretation of spiritual truth. God wants his children to prosper and live in good health.

'Beloved, I wish above all things that thou mayest prosper and be in health, even as thy soul prospereth'. 3 John 1:2 (KJV)

This book presents some practical secrets of wealth creation (accumulation) which break the cycle of poverty enslaving humanity. As you read this book, you are a few moments away from emancipating yourself from financial slavery.

I pray that may God of Heaven who gives ideas, wisdom and insight to make wealth with no added sorrows, to empower you with divine ideas and to prosper you spiritually and financially in the mighty name of Jesus after you read this book. Amen & Amen!

THE SECRET OF WEALTH CREATION

BREAKING THE CYCLE OF POVERTY

THINK carefully and reflectively about the scriptures below and pray for about five minutes before you continue to read.

THE SECRET OF WEALTH CREATION

BREAKING THE CYCLE OF POVERTY

> **Proverbs 10:15 (NLT)**
> *15. The wealth of the rich is their fortress; the poverty of the poor is their destruction.*

> **Ecclesiastes 7:12 (KJV)**
> *12. For wisdom is a defence, and money is a defence: but the excellency of knowledge is, that wisdom giveth life to them that have it.*

In this book, I have discussed THE 10 Ds OF SELF EMANCIPATION FROM FINANCIAL SLAVERY with some prayers and a saving plan that can help transform your financial status so that you can enjoy life to the full.

THE SECRET OF WEALTH CREATION: The D – FACTORS

> **Proverbs 24:33-34 (NLT)**
>
> *33. A little extra sleep, a little more slumber,*
>
>   *a little folding of the hands to rest—*
>
> *34. then poverty will pounce on you like a bandit;*
>
>   *scarcity will attack you like an armed robber.*

DISCOMFORT

The moment you realise that you are not comfortable with your financial status, you then have to think of creating something for yourself; after all, necessity is the mother of all inventions. This discomfort is evident when you are not happy with your job or finances and live on a restricted budget, living from hand to mouth just to make ends meet. Sometimes you are unable to pay your bills and keep borrowing from friends and relatives to pay for bills, personal or children's school/tuition fees and sometimes rent or travel expenses. When you find yourself living on credit cards and not debit cards you know that you are borrowing more than you can afford to pay back. In

THE SECRET OF WEALTH CREATION

BREAKING THE CYCLE OF POVERTY

effect, your life is running or is sustained only on credit.

The moment you see any of the above symptoms in your life, start to do something about it. Dream big, think big and create a mental picture of living in luxury or of escaping the bondage of poverty and scarcity. It is a challenging concept that requires careful thought and planning. The unpleasant and uncomfortable circumstances will provoke you to do something extraordinary to come out of the mess and shame of living in poverty. As a man thinks, so is he...... (Proverbs 23:7). Decide whether you want to remain in poverty or change your destiny by thinking reflectively and acting positively to break away. With diligence, a little planning, thinking, commitment, determination, perseverance and prayers, you will definitely break the ugly pattern of poverty in your generation.

DREAM

This type of dream is not the thoughts or sensations that go through a person's mind when asleep. It is rather the cherished aspiration, ambition or ideal (Oxford Dictionary). I mean a dream as a vision, a burning desire to create something new to make a difference. It is a dream to see yourself out of this dungeon, darkness, slavery, problem and lack of good things. One may ask: how can I do it? Imagine yourself overcoming this financial inadequacy and insufficiency. Make a concerted effort to create a mental picture of prosperity. Albert Einstein once said, *"I am enough of an artist to draw freely upon my imagination. Imagination is more important than knowledge. Knowledge is limited. Imagination encircles the world."*

Begin to apply what the Bible says in Joshua 1:8 by meditating and applying the word of God in your life and situations. Confess your greatness and believe in what you say.

THE SECRET OF WEALTH CREATION

BREAKING THE CYCLE OF POVERTY

Prayer - One

Father in the mighty name of Jesus,
I thank you that you have delivered me from every financial curse upon my life.
I thank you that you have broken any cycle of poverty confronting me.
I thank you that you have given me the power and authority to deliver myself from the shackles of poverty.
I take authority in the name of Jesus to root out, tear down, destroy and overthrow any spirit of poverty in my life.

Declaration

God of Abraham, Isaac and Jacob, in the mighty name of Jesus,
I thank you that you have given me power to build my finances and to plant my future in the name of Jesus.
I declare, in the name of God the Father, God the Son and God the Holy Spirit that I have come out of poverty.
I thank you, Lord for the ideas and wisdom you have given me to prosper in my finances in Jesus' name. Amen

THE SECRET OF WEALTH CREATION

BREAKING THE CYCLE OF POVERTY

> **Do not let this prayer be a nine-day-wonder. Persist in prayer in addition to your diligence and you can definitely change your situation in Jesus' name.**

DISCERNMENT

You cannot do it by your own efforts and works except through the power of the Holy Spirit who comes to calm down that storm of poverty. Desire the gift of discernment and God will bestow this gift in addition to others on you. The Bible says that even we human beings, if our children ask for food we do not give them stones, and when they ask for fish we do not give them snakes. This shows that if you desire to have any of the gifts of the Holy Spirit, God will give it to you according to his own will. Discernment is one of the gifts God gave to his children. This gift will enable you to distinguish between good and evil in order to spot the opportunities which human eyes would not otherwise fathom. The gift of discernment will point you to the right business to invest in and when to do so. This will quicken your understanding and creative abilities to stir up your sensitivity to spot opportunities in any given situation. You will be spiritually and physically alert to take advantage of opportunities. Your sensitivity to opportunities will be at the highest or optimal level. Pray for this gift and God will give you in His abundant provision. *(1 Cor 12:8-10)*

THE SECRET OF WEALTH CREATION

BREAKING THE CYCLE OF POVERTY

DIVINE DIRECTION

Pray to God in Jesus' name for divine direction. Divine direction is extremely crucial in life. The Bible says that we should commit all our ways to the Lord and not lean on our own understanding (Prov 3:5). God is the revealer of mysteries and the secret to prosperity. Let us lift up our hands and surrender to God that without Him we cannot do anything. Jesus said that without Him we can do nothing. Therefore, we must endeavour to abide with Him and His word in us (John 15:5). If the Lord Jesus becomes the master of our lives and we genuinely give Him the keys of our lives then we will not struggle in any area of our lives. Once we hand over our lives totally to the will of God, then we can boldly say that it is well with us because He will be the driver, captain, commander, pilot and the coach in our lives to drive us safely to our destinations and destinies.

Through divine direction, God will lead you to the still waters and the green pastures. He is indeed the source of your livelihood. Therefore, the problem of poverty and scarcity cannot prevail in His presence. He became poor for you to be rich. It is He who gives you the ability to produce wealth. You ought to accept and acknowledge what is yours and begin to enjoy life to the fullest. Jesus said, "I have come

THE SECRET OF WEALTH CREATION

BREAKING THE CYCLE OF POVERTY

for everyone to have life and have it more abundantly." Why then should some Christians live in abject poverty? This is a sign of ignorance and lack of knowledge because the Bible says my people perish for the lack of knowledge. This book is equipping you with insight about the secret of breaking the cycle of general poverty that confronts some children of God for their lack of knowledge and application of the word of God to situations that affect humanity.

Financial depravity is a harsh reality in our modern society. It confronts some children of God for lack of knowledge and application of word of God to situations that affect humanity. This book is going to equip you with powerful insight about the secret of breaking the cycle of poverty and to come out of the financial slavery to enjoy your life as God intended.

THE SECRET OF WEALTH CREATION

BREAKING THE CYCLE OF POVERTY

Prayer-Two

Father in the mighty name of Jesus,
I thank you that you have given me the gift of discernment to be able to spot opportunities and ideas to be successful in life. I thank you, heavenly Father that you have empowered me for greatness and success. I thank you, Lord for the divine direction you have given me.

As I continue to read this book, I pray that you give me insight and guide me beside the still waters and greener pastures in Jesus' name. Amen.

Father God of Abraham, Isaac and Jacob, you are a covenant-keeping God and you hasten to fulfil your word.

Today, in the name of Jesus, I take authority in your name and in the integrity of your word to root out, pull down, destroy and overthrow any satanic altars speaking against my finances. I root out, I pull down, I destroy and I overthrown any negative pronouncement against my finances in Jesus' name.

God the Father, God the Son, God the Holy Spirit, as I pray right now, I root out, I pull down, I destroy, and I overthrow any spiritual embargo and tax collectors on my finances in the name of Jesus. Amen.

THE SECRET OF WEALTH CREATION

BREAKING THE CYCLE OF POVERTY

Declaration

God of Abraham, Isaac and Jacob, in the mighty name of Jesus,
Today, I build my finances, in the name of Jesus.
I build my businesses in the name of Jesus.
I build my glory in the name of Jesus.
I plant financial blessing in the name of Jesus.
I plant my multi- billion dollar business to support the Kingdom of God and myself in the blessed name of Jesus.
I plant spirit of wisdom to be able to manage any money that comes into my hands in the name of Jesus. Amen.

Remember: God will not drop money from heaven to your bank account.

So learn a lesson from the scriptures below and do something to bring a change to your life and financial status.

Proverbs 6:5-11 (KJV)

5. Deliver thyself as a roe from the hand of the hunter, and as a bird from the hand of the fowler.

6. Go to the ant, thou sluggard; consider her ways, and be wise:

7. Which having no guide, overseer, or ruler,

8. Provideth her meat in the summer, and gathereth her food in the harvest.

9. How long wilt thou sleep, O sluggard? when wilt thou arise out of thy sleep?

> 10. Yet a little sleep, a little slumber, a little folding of the hands to sleep:
> 11. So shall thy poverty come as one that travelleth, and thy want as an armed man.
>
> **Persevere in prayers, apply wisdom and act on the word of God and you will see the change you desire to see in life.**

DISCIPLINE

This D-factor of wealth creation is the ability to transform your mindset not by conforming to the patterns of this world but rather by renewing your mind to trust in the Lord. Your faith in God with the renewed mind will enable you to enjoy the abundant life Jesus promised and to make your mark through your fulfilled life. Inasmuch as you believe in spiritual things, divine direction and supernatural breakthrough, God expects you to use the wisdom He has given you to excel in life.

We can simply begin to organise our lives by planning, budgeting, developing a saving plan and cutting down on unnecessary expenditures. This will help us live within our means in order to come out of living on a restricted budget. Coping with a limited budget has so many adverse effects on our lives. A low income is associated with some of the

THE SECRET OF WEALTH CREATION

BREAKING THE CYCLE OF POVERTY

following problems: stress, problems in marriages, disputes between family and relations, telling lies, health problems and loss of integrity and dignity. The Bible says that he who borrows becomes a slave to the lender.

Endeavour to learn how to plan, budget and undertake some personal money management or financial literacy courses to enable yourself to come out of financial bondage where necessary. Financial capabilities will help you liberate yourself from the cycle of poverty.

These financial management and capability skills will help you to disentangle yourself from financial oppression. Try to teach your children and the younger generation these financial emancipatory skills and secrets. The Bible says to teach the child the way s/he should go and s/he will not depart from it when s/he grows. These financial emancipatory skills will promote sustainability by instilling in children and young people the knowledge of how to break the cycle of poverty and financial insufficiency. Discourage young people from using credit cards, charge cards and store cards unnecessarily for daily expenses. They may only consider using these cards for business purposes and not for personal survival or as a last resort.

THE SECRET OF WEALTH CREATION

BREAKING THE CYCLE OF POVERTY

One practical step of coming out of debt is to have a **saving plan** because little drops of water make the mighty ocean. If you plan by taking care of the pennies, the pounds will certainly take care of themselves. **Develop the habit of saving. All it takes is discipline.** You cannot eat your cake and have it. If you cannot save with the little money that comes through your hands, it will be difficult to save regardless of how much you earn. What matters is how much you save and not how much you earn. I believe the simple saving plan below will ignite an inner yearning to save for the rainy day.

Saving Plan

This is the simple explanation of my saving plan. If you put **away/save** £1.00 (one pound) a day you would accumulate £365.00 (three hundred and sixty-five pounds) per annum. This is calculated as follows:

THE SECRET OF WEALTH CREATION

BREAKING THE CYCLE OF POVERTY

£1 Formular to Financial Freedom				
Daily Investment	1 Years Plan	3 Years Plan	5 Years Plan	10 Years Plan
£1	£365	£1,095	£1,825	£3
£2	£730	£2,190	£3,650	£7
£3	£1,095	£3,285	£5,475	£10
£4	£1,460	£4,380	£7,300	£14
£5	£1,825	£5,475	£9,125	£18
£6	£2,190	£6,570	£10,950	£21
£7	£2,555	£7,665	£12,775	£25
£8	£2,920	£8,760	£14,600	£29
£9	£3,285	£9,855	£16,425	£32
£10	£3,650	£10,950	£18,250	£36
£15	£5,475	£16,425	£27,375	£54
£20	£7,300	£21,900	£36,500	£73
£25	£9,125	£27,375	£45,625	£91
£30	£10,950	£32,850	£54,750	£109
£40	£14,600	£43,800	£73,000	£146
£50	£18,250	£54,750	£91,250	£182
£60	£21,900	£65,700	£109,500	£219
£70	£25,550	£76,650	£127,750	£255
£80	£29,200	£87,600	£146,000	£292
£90	£32,850	£98,550	£164,250	£328
£100	£36,500	£109,500	£182,500	£365
£200	£73,000	£219,000	£365,000	£730
£300	£109,500	£328,500	£547,500	£1,095
£400	£146,000	£438,000	£730,000	£1,460
£500	£182,500	£547,500	£912,500	£1,825
£1,000	£365,000	£1,095,000	£1,825,000	£3,650
£5,000	£1,825,000	£5,475,000	£9,125,000	£18,250

THE SECRET OF WEALTH CREATION

BREAKING THE CYCLE OF POVERTY

This simple saving scheme will be your first attempt to come out of a financial burden. You can practise this plan without feeling that you are taking money out of your limited budget. Although the amount you accumulate looks small, remember that little drops of water make the mighty ocean. If you do not respect small money, big money will not respect you too since respect is reciprocal. Begin to respect money and money will respect you. You may want to invest this money annually in some viable ventures. At the worst, deposit it in a savings account or in your ISA where the money will not be taxed but rather attract at least some infinitesimal interest. After all, half a loaf is better than none.

A journey of one thousand miles begins with the very first step. Why not start by using a shoe box, perfume box or any container and drop a pound in on a daily basis. Preferably deposit it in your money box weekly; however, if you are paid monthly then endeavour to save monthly. Please do not **procrastinate** on your monthly deposits. Procrastination is the thief of time. Act now to liberate yourself from hardship. Procrastination leads to 'Had I known' and 'Had I known' is also the philosophy of a fool. Time and tides wait for nobody. Begin to act **NOW.** There is no best time than **NOW.** Ask God fervently **NOW** to lead you and

THE SECRET OF WEALTH CREATION

BREAKING THE CYCLE OF POVERTY

be with you in your attempt to take the first step in your saving plan.

This saving plan is similar to what Apostle Paul offered the people of Corinth in order to save money for the people of Jerusalem by putting aside some money weekly. It is mind-blowing to realise how much you can accrue a short length of time. In this way, you don't feel that you are parting with money as compared to waiting to save monthly or a longer duration where you will experience the burden of putting aside a bigger chunk of money. Strive to practise this EVERY WEEK in order to produce a fruitful result.

On the first day of every week, each one of you should set aside a sum of money in keeping with his income, saving it up, so that when I come no collections will have to be made.
1 Corinthians 16:2 (NIV)

Better still, you may as well set up a standing order to your saving account. However, be careful not to fall a victim of paying bank charges for unauthorised borrowing. If care is not taken you may be penalised which will worsen your circumstances and you will feel as if you are jumping from the frying pan into the fire, by paying £28 to £35 bank charges for the £1 or £10 standing order.

THE SECRET OF WEALTH CREATION

BREAKING THE CYCLE OF POVERTY

Let us consider how much we can save when we put aside £2.00 a day for a rainy day. If you do not plan to save, then it signifies that you are ready to live in poverty or on a restricted budget. The Bible admonishes us to be wise in saving as this is typified in Proverbs 6:6-8 (NLT)

6. Take a lesson from the ants, you lazybones. Learn from their ways and become wise!

7. Though they have no prince or governor or ruler to make them work,

8. they labour hard all summer, gathering food for the winter.

Make an effort to put a little aside while there is the opportunity because one has to make hay whilst the sun shines and strike when the iron is hot. The table above shows how much you can save when you go an extra mile to put £2.00 a day.

You can use this saving scheme with any currency and either increase or decrease the daily deposit to what suits you.

The saving modality with any amount is applicable to strategies under a one pound saving plan.

Everybody can use this saving strategy to build up funds. Both children and adults can practise this saving plan. Children and young adults can save part of the money given to them by their parents or relatives on their birthdays and festive occasions to join the saving scheme.

DETERMINATION

Determination is a characteristic every successful person must exhibit. Determination is fixing your eyes on the destination. You must focus on your destination, your dream and where you want to be in life without giving up. In other words, do not let anything else distract you from your ultimate goal and purpose in life.

We find in the Bible many achievers who exhibited this enterprising characteristic in their lives. They continued in their pursuits with perseverance until they had achieved what they wanted in life. Two such people are the Prophet Elisha and Ruth.

Firstly, Prophet Elisha accepted the calling of God and followed Elijah until he received the double portion of Elijah's anointing from the Lord. Elijah tried all means to persuade Elisha not to follow him. Elisha became a great achiever and God powerfully used him to accomplish two times the miracles of his master Elijah.

THE SECRET OF WEALTH CREATION

BREAKING THE CYCLE OF POVERTY

Secondly, Ruth became a widow but decided to follow Naomi to maintain the relationship even unto death, regardless of Naomi's attempts to persuade her to return to her family. Ruth was so determined that nothing could persuade her to turn back until she finally re-married Boaz, a multi-millionaire.

Elisha's determination gained him double portion of Elijah's anointing and Ruth's determination gained her multitudes of blessings. Many people give up too soon. If Elisha turned back when Elijah asked him three times to go back and to leave him alone, he could not have been blessed with a double portion anointing. (1 Kings 19: 16-21 through to 2 Kings 2:1-22)

If Ruth had returned to her family after Naomi persistently asked her to do so, she would not have received the reward and the blessing she enjoyed in the latter days of her life. (Ruth chapters 1 to 4).

Everybody wants a double portion of blessings but not everyone is prepared to go that extra mile due to the price to pay or challenges and problems. Perseverance conquers all difficulties so continue until you have received reward and result for your efforts.

THE SECRET OF WEALTH CREATION

BREAKING THE CYCLE OF POVERTY

Ruth's determination: Read the book of Ruth.

The Bible says in 1 Thessalonians 4:11-12, NIV that you should determine to achieve something in life by minding your own business and by working with your hands. The scripture below clearly signifies that you can only deliver yourself from what you are not happy with by being creative to work with your hands. It is not anybody's hands but your own. If you read the book of Exodus, you will notice how mightily God has blessed our hands. God has put everything we need to succeed in life in our hands. Moses used what was in his hands to do so many miracles to bring glory to God. When Moses was in doubt whether or not the people of Israel would believe in him that he had indeed had an encounter with God. God used the staff Moses had in his hands (Exodus 4:2-7). If you identify what you have in your hands, then God will use it to bless you.

The following are some examples of how God blessed people for what they had in their hands/house.

2 Kings 4:1-7 (NLT)
Elisha Helps a Poor Widow

1. One day the widow of a member of the group of prophets came to Elisha and cried out, "My husband who served you is dead, and you know how he feared the LORD. But now a creditor has come, threatening to take my two sons as slaves."

THE SECRET OF WEALTH CREATION

BREAKING THE CYCLE OF POVERTY

> 2. "What can I do to help you?" Elisha asked. "Tell me, what do you have in the house?"
> "Nothing at all, except a flask of olive oil," she replied.
> 3. And Elisha said, "Borrow as many empty jars as you can from your friends and neighbours.
> 4. Then go into your house with your sons and shut the door behind you. Pour olive oil from your flask into the jars, setting each one aside when it is filled."
> 5. So she did as she was told. Her sons kept bringing jars to her, and she filled one after another.
> 6. Soon every container was full to the brim!
> "Bring me another jar," she said to one of her sons.
> "There aren't any more!" he told her. And then the olive oil stopped flowing.
> 7. When she told the man of God what had happened, he said to her, "Now sell the olive oil and pay your debts, and you and your sons can live on what is left over."

God used the little oil the widow had to get her out of debt. Whatever you need to come out of debt is in your hands. What is your talent, gift, or potential? Find your talents, what you are good at and enjoy doing without getting bored or tired. Your debt will not go away, so deal with it.

THE SECRET OF WEALTH CREATION

BREAKING THE CYCLE OF POVERTY

Again, the widow of Zarephath also had only a handful of flour in a jar and a little oil in a jug. God blessed the little she had. (1 Kings 17:7-16).

The Bible admonishes us to work hard to be successful and have a vision to be independent as Paul indicated in 1 Thessalonians 4:11-12) NIV. 11. Make it your ambition to lead a quiet life, to mind your own business and to work with your hands, just as we told you,

12. so that your daily life may win the respect of outsiders and so that you will not be dependent on anybody.

The Bible also requires from us to do whatever we find to do with diligence.

You may be a good cook; think of turning it into a business. Maybe you are a teacher and so do something with your skills by organising some private tuition or evening and after school clubs. If your capacity cannot permit you to execute your dreams alone, you could join hands with other people to establish your idea. Many hands make light work. You may be a good communicator full of wisdom and humour. Why can't you develop this gift into a consultancy/counselling firm? *You could write books or poems in order to turn your dreams into a reality. Whatever you are good at or love to do can be transformed into a business venture.* Our Lord Jesus

THE SECRET OF WEALTH CREATION

BREAKING THE CYCLE OF POVERTY

Christ demonstrated entrepreneurial skills and enterprising capabilities in His daily routine. He woke up early in the morning to pray every day. He worked long hours, without complaining, to the extent that some of His disciples became hungry and exhausted. When the people became hungry, He could have just prayed to call food from heaven to feed them. However, since He wanted to prove to us the power of what we have in our hands, he requested for any food in anybody's hands. It happened that a young boy had two fishes and three loaves of bread. Once Jesus had this in his hands, He lifted it to heaven and blessed it and the Bible declares that there was an overflow of food. There was a surplus after feeding the five thousand men. I believe there were women and children who were not counted. Can you identify your gift, talents or what is in your hands? Once you have identified it that will mark the beginning of your greatness. What do you have in your hands?

Also, His entrepreneurship was clearly evident in the parable of the talents.

> **Matthew 25:14-30 (NIV)**
> ***The Parable of the Talents***
> 14."Again, it will be like a man going on a journey, who called his servants and entrusted his property to them.

15. To one he gave five talents of money, to another two talents, and to another one talent, each according to his ability. Then he went on his journey.

16. The man who had received the five talents went at once and put his money to work and gained five more.

17. So also, the one with the two talents gained two more. [18]But the man who had received the one talent went off, dug a hole in the ground and hid his master's money.

19. "After a long time the master of those servants returned and settled accounts with them.

*20. **The man who had received the five talents brought the other five. 'Master,' he said, 'you entrusted me with five talents. See, I have gained five more.'***

21. "His master replied, 'Well done, good and faithful servant! You have been faithful with a few things; I will put you in charge of many things. Come and share your master's happiness!'

*22. **"The man with the two talents also came. 'Master,' he said, 'you entrusted me with two talents; see, I have gained two more.'***

23. "His master replied, 'Well done, good and faithful servant! You have been faithful with a few things; I will put you in charge of many things. Come and share your master's happiness!'

24. "Then the man who had received the one talent came. 'Master,' he said, 'I knew that you are a hard man, harvesting where you have not sown and

THE SECRET OF WEALTH CREATION

BREAKING THE CYCLE OF POVERTY

> gathering where you have not scattered seed. *25. **So I was afraid and went out and hid your talent in the ground. See, here is what belongs to you.***'
> 26. "His master replied, 'You wicked, lazy servant! So you knew that I harvest where I have not sown and gather where I have not scattered seed?
> 27. Well then, you should have put my money on deposit with the bankers, so that when I returned I would have received it back with interest.
> 28. " 'Take the talent from him and give it to the one who has the ten talents.
> 29. For everyone who has will be given more, and he will have an abundance. Whoever does not have, **even what he has will be taken from him**. 30. And throw that worthless servant outside, into the darkness, where there will be weeping and gnashing of teeth.'

It is obvious from the above passage that our Lord Jesus Christ was teaching proper economics and business. Entrepreneurship and enterprising skills should be part and parcel of our Christian walk and work to think creatively. God has put diverse gifts and talents in every person. It is up to the individuals either to activate and develop their talents or bury their potentials and blame others for their failures. The fact that you have a little does not mean that you cannot succeed.

THE SECRET OF WEALTH CREATION

BREAKING THE CYCLE OF POVERTY

However, the person who received two talents as well as the five applied wisdom to increase them whereas the man with the one talent buried it because of unnecessary criticism, jealousy and unjustifiable accusations of his master.

Eventually, he lost the little he had because he did not make use of what he had in his hands. Remember, whatever your hands can do, do it well with all your might and industriousness, knowledge, planning and wisdom whilst you are still alive. Strive to make a difference and excel in whatever you do to be a blessing to others. Perseverance conquers difficulties. Determine to succeed and you can make it. Do not quit because quitters do not win.

I have seen real application of the Matthew 25:29 in our societies. The Bible says everyone who has will be given more and has in abundance but for whoever does not have, even what he has will be taken from him. This is what is happening in the banks where those who do not have much are mostly unfairly being charged penalties for unauthorised borrowing. Sometimes you may have a standing order/direct debit of say £15.00, but because that person does not have much; they end up paying fines and charges ranging from £28 to £35 for their inability to have enough funds in their account to settle for the £15 pounds standing order.

THE SECRET OF WEALTH CREATION

BREAKING THE CYCLE OF POVERTY

In some instances, one has to pay for the penalty say £35 pounds plus the £15 standing order and occasionally, some company may also charge you a late payment and the reinstatement of direct debit fees.

I have suffered this and I know what I am talking about. However, it is needless to say that those who have more money sitting in their account will definitely attract at least some interest as Jesus clearly illustrated in Matthew 25: 27. The master expected the servant with the one talent to have **at least** deposited/invested money in the bank to attract some interest. Matthew 25:27 (NLT)
27. why didn't you deposit my money in the bank? At least I could have gotten some interest on it.'

Those who are against prosperity messages should carefully read the parable of the talent to have a transformed mind. Begin to think as an entrepreneur, dream of having your own business and living a successful life and reaching out to your communities. Aspire to become a financial evangelist or kingdom of God financier.

THE SECRET OF WEALTH CREATION

BREAKING THE CYCLE OF POVERTY

Prayer - Three

Father in the mighty name of Jesus,

Today, I thank you for the wisdom and the ability you have given to me in the name of your son Jesus to change my destiny by the creative words in my mouth.

Your word says in the book of Jeremiah that you have today, set me over nations and kingdoms, to pluck up, and to break down, and to destroy and to overthrow anything in my life that I do not want or approve.

By the power of the Holy Ghost, today,

I pluck up, break down, destroy and overthrow any altar or stronghold from my parental lineage, from my friends, work colleagues, matrimonial home, my church that is speaking against my finances in the name of Jesus Christ of Nazareth.

In the name of Jesus, I command any demonic tax collector in my life to die by the fire of the Holy Ghost,

Holy Ghost, you are the consuming fire, I pray in the name of Jesus that you consume any spiritual tax force, or levy on my finances.

In the name of Jesus, whatsoever, against my finances and prosperity must die by the fire of the Holy Ghost .Father in the name of Jesus, whosoever has done anything against my finances and

THE SECRET OF WEALTH CREATION

BREAKING THE CYCLE OF POVERTY

prosperity must die by the fire of the Holy Ghost.

Declaration

God of Abraham, Isaac and Jacob, you are the merciful father and a gracious God. Forgive me my sins, transgression, trespasses and iniquities by showing me mercy.

I thank you in the mighty name of Jesus that today you have delivered me from any financial limitation and scarcity.

Your word says that it is you who give me the ability, strength, wisdom, empowerment and enablement to make wealth.

I thank you that I have received supernatural wisdom to make wealth. Father, in the name of Jesus, I thank you that you have equipped me with the secret to make wealth.

Today, I build my finances, in the name of Jesus.

I build my businesses in the name of Jesus.

I build my glory in the name of Jesus.

I plant financial blessing in the name of Jesus.

I plant my multi billion business to support the Kingdom of God and myself in the blessed name of Jesus.

I plant spirit of wisdom to be able to manage any money that comes into my hands in the name of Jesus. Amen.

Remember: God will not drop money from heaven to your bank account.

Study carefully the scripture below. Meditate on it

and use it to pray diligently and persistently and God will answer your prayers to make you prosperous and successful in the mighty name of Jesus.

Joshua 1:8 *(KJV)*

⁸This book of the law shall not depart out of thy mouth; but thou shalt meditate therein day and night, that thou mayest observe to do according to all that is written therein: for then thou shalt make thy way prosperous, and then thou shalt have good success.

Persevere in prayers, apply wisdom and act on the word of God and you will see the change you desire to see in life.

Proverbs 6:10-11 *(NIVUK)*

10. A little sleep, a little slumber, a little folding of the hands to rest –

11. and poverty will come on you like a thief and scarcity like an armed man.

DILIGENCE

This D - factor of financial emancipation is the willpower and the zeal to succeed. Nobody can change your destiny other than **YOU**. As the saying goes, you can force a horse to the riverside but cannot force it to drink. People can give you all sorts of advice and support but if you

THE SECRET OF WEALTH CREATION

BREAKING THE CYCLE OF POVERTY

are not willing to help yourself, all efforts will be futile. You can receive all forms of prayers and deliverances but if you do not do anything about the physical aspect of life, all efforts will prove fruitless.

You should always aspire to go an extra mile in everything you do. This can be exhibited in your work life, church life and family life. If you exercise diligence in whatever you do, the reward will be remarkable.

With all the afore-discussed D- factors: discomfort, dream, discern, divine direction, discipline coupled with diligence you can break every yoke that ties you to poverty. With diligence and prayer every mountain of poverty shall be levelled and removed. Delays cannot prevail; failure at the edge of success cannot triumph over success and victory. Some people become poor because of laziness and flimsy excuses. The Bible clearly exemplifies this by scriptures below and many more.

Proverbs 10:4-5 (NIV)
4. Lazy hands make a man poor, but diligent hands bring wealth.
5. He who gathers crops in summer is a wise son, but he who sleeps during harvest is a disgraceful son

THE SECRET OF WEALTH CREATION

BREAKING THE CYCLE OF POVERTY

Proverbs 20:13 (NLT)

*13. If you love sleep, you will end in poverty.
Keep your eyes open, and there will be plenty to eat!*

Proverbs 24:30-34 (NLT)

30. I walked by the field of a lazy person, the vineyard of one with no common sense.
31. I saw that it was overgrown with nettles. It was covered with weeds,
and its walls were broken down.
*32. Then, as I looked and thought about it,
I learned this lesson:*
*33. A little extra sleep, a little more slumber,
a little folding of the hands to rest —*
34. then poverty will pounce on you like a bandit; scarcity

THE SECRET OF WEALTH CREATION

BREAKING THE CYCLE OF POVERTY

Proverbs 6:6-11 (NLT)

6. *Take a lesson from the ants, you lazybones. Learn from their ways and become wise!*
7. *Though they have no prince or governor or ruler to make them work,*
8. *they labour hard all summer, gathering food for the winter.*
9. *But you, lazybones, how long will you sleep? When will you wake up?*
10. *A little extra sleep, a little more slumber, a little folding of the hands to rest—*
11. *then poverty will pounce on you like a bandit; scarcity will attack you like an armed robber.*

All the above scriptures are all talking about laziness. Let us learn a lesson from the end result of laziness. My seven-year-old son once said to his mum that *'a man does not sleep in the afternoon',* when he was asked to have a nap. His explanation was he had a lot of things to do. The message here is that if a seven year old boy knows the consequences of too much sleeping, how much more an adult should be aware of about wasting time and the results thereof. This is honestly like what Proverbs 20:13 says. If you love sleep, you will end up in poverty. It further states 'keep your eyes open and there will be plenty to eat'! As an entrepreneur you must be able to spot the opportunities others cannot see.

Many people waste precious time by not dealing with their own attitude, character and behaviour. Instead of using their time profitably to develop themselves, they rather spend **a little time** gossiping, **a little time** chatting on telephone, **a little time** surfing the net, Facebook, MSN, Skype, Whatsapp, **a little time** grumbling, **a little time** watching television, movies and later blame others for their mistakes.

Identify your weaknesses and areas that need to be improved by finding the right strategies to develop yourself in order to pounce on poverty, breaking its sting in your life to live a fulfilled life for yourself and others.

A little more reading, search of knowledge, advice, good counsel, productive networking, planning your life, setting goals and targets in life, assessing and evaluating your life, reduction of lengthy conversations and above all a little more praying will lift you out of poverty. You can pounce on poverty like a bandit and attack scarcity like an armed robber. **YOU** and only **YOU** can deliver yourself and be the change agent to bring about a better and prosperous life.

THE SECRET OF WEALTH CREATION

BREAKING THE CYCLE OF POVERTY

> ***Proverbs 19:15, 24***
> *15. Lazy people sleep soundly,*
> *but idleness leaves them hungry.*
> *24. Lazy people take food in their hand*
> *but don't even lift it to their mouth.*

The book of proverbs talks more about the laziness and idleness. Let us learn to be diligent in whatever we do. Laziness breeds poverty whereas diligence brings prosperity and abundance of blessing.

DISCOVERY

The discovery of your talent, skills and abilities can only happen when you decide to spend some time inquiring from the Lord and through the study of His word. Sometimes the discovery can come through dreams, visions, revelations and prophetic utterances. The Bible says we have to study to get ourselves approved. Once you have identified your talents and gifts you need to invest time to develop them.

Another discovery exercise can be to spend time thinking carefully about your strengths and weakness. You can do this by talking to people around you or finding out what you love to do without being told to do so, or what you enjoy doing whether paid or unpaid. There are some occasions you may have to study and train yourself by investing time, money and resources into developing your skills to find out the real self in you.

DEVELOPMENT

The Bible declares in 2 Timothy 2:15 that you should study to get yourself approved. This implies therefore that you should not sit down to put your hands on your laps expecting God to rain money, food, clothing, shoes, job and even fill job application forms from heaven to you. DO SOMETHING about your situation by developing yourself to deliver yourself from financial slavery by applying the word of God to any problem of limitation that confronts you.

This verse starts with a command 'study

"Study to show yourself approved to God, a workman that needs not to be ashamed, rightly dividing the word of truth" 2 Timothy 2:15 (American King James Version)

Under this heading, we will consider only two types of development:

THE SECRET OF WEALTH CREATION

BREAKING THE CYCLE OF POVERTY

Self and Business

In the first place, you will need to develop yourself by one of the following:

Self Development
- ✓ Education
- ✓ Studies
- ✓ Research
- ✓ Online self-learning
- ✓ Self-directed learning
- ✓ Seminars
- ✓ Networking
- ✓ Reading
- ✓ Talking to people in similar field, trade, profession or business you want to go into.

Business development

Here, you develop your business idea into a profitable and tangible business.
- ✓ You can develop your stationery, business cards, letterhead, complimentary slips, leaflets and flyers.
- ✓ Purchase domain name
- ✓ Open bank account when possible
- ✓ Test product/service with friend and family when applicable
- ✓ You can write your business plan
- ✓ Marketing and promotion

THE SECRET OF WEALTH CREATION

BREAKING THE CYCLE OF POVERTY

Once you have the above in place, then you have to make conscious effort to be abreast with your business product or service, inside out, to persuasively present your idea in one to two minutes. Imagine you meet someone (potential customer, client or investors) in a lift from the ground floor to the tenth floor; can you convincingly present or sell your business to the fellow and compel him/her to ask for your business card or to arrange a meeting? If you can answer yes to the above then you are ready for action. The process of presenting your business idea or proposal within the shortest possible time and lure your listeners or audience is called an elevator pitch.

You can pitch your idea or business succinctly to secure funding or finance to start or grow your business.

Sources of finance:
Below are some useful tips for generating income for your business:

Own income or savings
The whole concept of this book is to help readers save money, come out of poverty and take control of their finances. You can plan to save for a specified period of time in order to gain some money to start your business. This is the most

THE SECRET OF WEALTH CREATION

BREAKING THE CYCLE OF POVERTY

effective way of generating or getting finance to start your business. You can decide to save for one, two or three years in order to build some finance to take your business off the ground.

Family and friends

In this economic crisis, it is also easy and practical to raise some funds from family and friends. People will give to support your vision if they find you trustworthy and they are certain that they will get their money back. At any time in life, regardless of the state of the economy, there are some people who have some money and looking for great opportunity or a genuine reason to spend their money. You can pitch your idea or business to your family and friends to raise some money to support you to start your business. However, be careful your idea is not taken by anyone in your attempt to secure funding for your business. Try to have some safeguarding mechanism in place to prevent your idea from being stolen.

Partnership or shares with family or friends

Another good and effective way to generate finance to start your business is to consider partnership or selling shares to family and friends.

There are some family members or friends who have money but will not be willing to give you as a loan. Such people prefer to have a share or stake in

THE SECRET OF WEALTH CREATION

BREAKING THE CYCLE OF POVERTY

the business. In this case, try to have some contract or terms and conditions in place to safeguard your business and idea.

Depending on the type of business and how much you can inject into the family, you can float some shares to family members or friends who may be willing to be part of the business.

THE SECRET OF WEALTH CREATION

BREAKING THE CYCLE OF POVERTY

Type	You	Friend/family 1	Friend/family 2	Friend/family 3
A	70%	10%	10%	10%
	70%	30%	-	-
B	60%	20%	10%	10%
	60%	40%	-	-
C	50%	20%	20%	10%
	50%	50%	-	-
D	40%	20%	20%	20%
	40%	60%	-	-

From the above table, depending on your financial strength, you can decide to adopt any of the types A-D. You can hold 70 percent and float 30 percent to one person as a partner or three persons considering the interest of family and friends around you. The same goes with the other types (B, C & D).

Investors

Investors can also sometimes dictate their terms and conditions with a similar pattern of investment applying the chart below.

Type	You	Investor
A	70%	30%
	30%	70%
B	60%	40%
	40%	60%

THE SECRET OF WEALTH CREATION

BREAKING THE CYCLE OF POVERTY

C	50%	50%

Bank
Finally, you can get a loan from a bank depending on your credit worthiness and your business plan.

Examples of some Bible entrepreneurs

Examples of some Bible entrepreneurs	
Old Testament	New Testament
Abraham & Lot (Gen 13)	Jesus-Carpenter,
Isaac (Gen 26:1-34)	Luke (Col 4:14)
Jacob (Gen 30:31-43)	Paul, Priscilla and
Joseph (Gen 41:33-46)	Aquila-Tentmakers
Solomon (1 Kings 10: 14-29)	(Acts 18:1-3)
Job (Job 1:3, 42:10-12)	Lydia- (Acts 16:14)
Boaz: (Ruth 2:1- 9)	Peter & Andrew- (Matthew 4:18)

THE SECRET OF WEALTH CREATION

BREAKING THE CYCLE OF POVERTY

DIRECTORSHIP

It is the will of God that His children prosper in everything (businesses, health, marriage, education, child bearing) and excel in all areas of life. This assurance can be seen in 3 John 1:2, "Beloved, I pray that you may prosper in all things and be in health, just as your soul prospers" (NKJV).

It can be seen from the above scripture that God is interested and concerned about our welfare and wellbeing. Therefore if you decide to come out of poverty, God will bless you to be successful since His word has promised that He wants us to prosper in everything that pertains to life that we lay our hands on.

Do something and the God of Abraham, Isaac and Jacob will bless the work of your hands. DO SOMETHING about your situation now and stop blaming people for your mistakes. Complaining, making excuses, or blaming others for your problems will not compensate your poverty for riches or wealth.

Below are some examples of business men and women (entrepreneurs) in the Bible.

THE SECRET OF WEALTH CREATION

BREAKING THE CYCLE OF POVERTY

You can also become a successful businessperson or a successful entrepreneur to support the Kingdom of God, the needy and yourself.

To prove that you really want to change your situation by breaking the cycle of poverty, you should spend some time to read all the scriptures about the successful rich Bible personalities in the table above and do the exercises below:

- Read each scripture carefully and prayerfully.
- Meditate on each passage
- Read it again
- Then write the type of work or profession and list at least three enterprising and entrepreneurial characteristics of each individual
- I strongly believe that by the time you finish this exercise you will be stirred up and be ready for success.
- Finally, state and explain any three characteristics you possess and how you intend to use them in your business endeavours.

Some Old Testament Rich & Wealthy People
Abraham & Lot (Gen 13)

THE SECRET OF WEALTH CREATION

BREAKING THE CYCLE OF POVERTY

Isaac (Gen 26:1-34)

Jacob (Gen 30:31 – 43)

Joseph (Gen 41:33-46)

Solomon (1 Kings 10:14-29)

THE SECRET OF WEALTH CREATION

BREAKING THE CYCLE OF POVERTY

Job (Job 1:3, 42:10-12)

Boaz: (Ruth 2:1;9)

State and explain any three characteristics you possess and how you intend to use them in your business endeavours.

THE SECRET OF WEALTH CREATION

BREAKING THE CYCLE OF POVERTY

Some New Testament Rich & Wealthy People

Luke (Col 4:14)

Paul, Priscilla and Aquila (Acts 18:1-3)

Lydia - (Acts 16:14)

Peter & Andrew – (Matthew 4:18)

THE SECRET OF WEALTH CREATION

BREAKING THE CYCLE OF POVERTY

State and explain any three characteristics you possess and how you intend to use them in your business endeavours.

Take control of your life and business and make the decision to sustain and improve your business.

'You are the head and not the tail'. Take your position and activate/initiate your leadership skills. Below are some leadership skills and entrepreneurial characteristics you need to exhibit and demonstrate in your directorship (your day-to-day dealings).

THE SECRET OF WEALTH CREATION

BREAKING THE CYCLE OF POVERTY

Enterprise & Entrepreneurial Skills and Characteristics

Vision & Purpose	Creativity/ innovation
Drive	Motivation
Risk taking	Commitment/Dedication
Confidence	Communication/ Negotiation
Perseverance	Organisation
Determination	Action- orientated
Adaptability	Focused
Passionate	Resilient
Persuasiveness	Initiative

THE SECRET OF WEALTH CREATION

BREAKING THE CYCLE OF POVERTY

Prayer – Four

Now thank God for wisdom and ideas He has bestowed on you by reading this book.
Father in the mighty name of Jesus,
Today, I thank you for the wisdom and the ability you have given to me in the name of your son Jesus to change my destiny by the creative words in my mouth.
Father, I thank you that you rooted out, pulled down, destroyed and thrown down any spirit of limitation, hardship, unfruitfulness, failures and delays affecting my life.
In the mighty name of Jesus I have prayed.

Declaration
God of Abraham, Isaac and Jacob, you are the merciful father and a gracious God. I am victorious in the name of Jesus.
I am more than a conqueror in the name of Jesus.
I am a success in the name of Jesus.
I shall not lack anything in the name of Jesus for my God will supply all my needs, according to his glorious riches in Christ Jesus.
I shall not borrow but I will lend to nations because God has given me the power to build and to plant my finances in the name of Jesus Christ of Nazareth.
Father, in the name of Jesus, I thank you for the creative and innovative ideas, knowledge, gifts, wisdom and talent to transform my financial

THE SECRET OF WEALTH CREATION

BREAKING THE CYCLE OF POVERTY

position in the name of the Father, the Son and the Holy Spirit.

Remember: God will not drop money from heaven to your bank account.
Study carefully the scripture below. Meditate on it and use it to pray diligently and persistently and God will answer your prayers to make you prosperous and successful in the mighty name of Jesus.
Proverbs 22:7(KJV)
7. The rich ruleth over the poor, and the borrower is servant to the lender.
Persevere in prayers, apply wisdom and act on the word of God and you will see the change you desire to see in life.
I hope you have been provoked by Proverbs 22:7 and you are ready to take action.
It is now your time to act on all the inspiration you have read from this book.
ACT NOW!!! ACTION! ACTION!! ACTION!!!

THE SECRET OF WEALTH CREATION

BREAKING THE CYCLE OF POVERTY

Entrepreneurship and Business Idea Generation Exercise

For the sake of those who may not have the Bible with you at the time of reading this book of wealth creation, I have taken the pain to produce the scriptures below to enable you to do this exercise. This book is yours so feel free to make notes as you read on:

What five different business ideas you can get after reading the scriptures below:

THE SECRET OF WEALTH CREATION

BREAKING THE CYCLE OF POVERTY

Job 1:3 (NLT)
3. He owned 7,000 sheep, 3,000 camels, 500 teams of oxen, and 500 female donkeys. He also had many servants. He was, in fact, the richest person in that entire area.

Job 42:10-12 (NLT)
10. When Job prayed for his friends, the LORD restored his fortunes. In fact, the LORD gave him twice as much as before!
11. Then all his brothers, sisters, and former friends came and feasted with him in his home. And they consoled him and comforted him because of all the trials the LORD had brought against him. And each of them brought him a gift of money and a gold ring.
12. So the LORD blessed Job in the second half of his life even more than in the beginning. For now he had 14,000 sheep, 6,000 camels, 1,000 teams of oxen, and 1,000 female donkeys.

State five business ideas

1.

2.

3.

4.

5.

THE SECRET OF WEALTH CREATION

BREAKING THE CYCLE OF POVERTY

Acts 18:3 (NLT)
3. Paul lived and worked with them, for they were tentmakers just as he was

Acts 16:14 (NLT)
14. One of them was Lydia from Thyatira, a merchant of expensive purple cloth, who worshiped God. As she listened to us, the Lord opened her heart, and she accepted what Paul was saying.

State five business ideas

1.

2.

3.

4.

5.

THE SECRET OF WEALTH CREATION

BREAKING THE CYCLE OF POVERTY

Matthew 4:18 (NLT)
18. One day as Jesus was walking along the shore of the Sea of Galilee, he saw two brothers—Simon, also called Peter, and Andrew—throwing a net into the water, for they fished for a living.

Bezalel and Oholiab

Exodus 35:30-35 (NLT)
30. Then Moses told the people of Israel, "The LORD has specifically chosen Bezalel son of Uri, grandson of Hur, of the tribe of Judah.

31. The LORD has filled Bezalel with the Spirit of God, giving him great wisdom, ability, and expertise in all kinds of crafts.

32. He is a master craftsman, expert in working with gold, silver, and bronze.

33. He is skilled in engraving and mounting gemstones and in carving wood. He is a master at every craft.

34. And the LORD has given both him and Oholiab son of Ahisamach, of the tribe of Dan, the ability to teach their skills to others.

35. The LORD has given them special skills as engravers, designers, embroiderers in blue, purple, and scarlet thread on fine linen cloth, and weavers. They excel as craftsmen and as designers.

State five business ideas

1.

2.

THE SECRET OF WEALTH CREATION

BREAKING THE CYCLE OF POVERTY

3.

4.

5.

THE SECRET OF WEALTH CREATION

BREAKING THE CYCLE OF POVERTY

Prayer – Five

Invitation to Jesus Christ
Read the following scriptures intently and act on it.
Romans 10:9-12 (NLT)

9. If you confess with your mouth that Jesus is Lord and believe in your heart that God raised him from the dead, you will be saved.

10. For it is by believing in your heart that you are made right with God, and it is by confessing with your mouth that you are saved.

11. As the Scriptures tell us, "Anyone who trusts in him will never be disgraced.

If you do not know Jesus Christ as your Lord and personal saviour, then I will urge you to humbly give him your life and let Him take charge of everything of your life NOW and FOREVER.

PRAY the PRAYER below out loud.

Lord Jesus Christ of Nazareth, Today I give you my life, mind, body, and soul.

I believe in my heart and confess with my mouth that you are the son of the Living God. I believe that you came to die for my sins, transgressions, trespasses and iniquities. I believe that God raised you from the dead and you are now seated in Glory on the right hand side of God interceding for me.

Lord Jesus, I thank you that you have come into my life and made all things new in me. I confess that I am saved and have become new because the old

things have passed away. In Jesus' name. Amen.

THE SECRET OF WEALTH CREATION

BREAKING THE CYCLE OF POVERTY

Other Publications

1. *Dream Activator*
2. Six Secrets of Total Deliverance & Success
3. TESTMONY OR TESTMONEY: *Pass the Test and Get the Money*
4. *Baptism: Choice or Command? FIND OUT!*
5. *My Calling and Elisha's Calling: Evidence and Signals Unnoticed.*
6. *Praising God Through Wilderness: Staying Safe During Wilderness Experience*
7. The Three Wisdom Keys
8. Get The Formula Right
9. Decision Time Children' Series: Anger

THE SECRET OF WEALTH CREATION

BREAKING THE CYCLE OF POVERTY

ABOUT THE BOOK

Many people are suffering financially and are struggling to come out of it. Some are able to come out of financial mess but others are drowned in it for ever. Some people are born into poverty and it becomes a problem that fights them from generations to generations.

This book presents some practical secrets of wealth creation which break the cycle of poverty that enslaves humanity. As you read this book, you are few moments away from emancipating yourself from financial slavery.

I pray that may God of Heaven who gives ideas, wisdom and insight to make wealth with no added sorrows empower you with divine ideas to prosper spiritually and financially after reading this book in the mighty name of Jesus. Amen & Amen!

THE SECRET OF WEALTH CREATION

BREAKING THE CYCLE OF POVERTY

ABOUT THE AUTHOR

Paapa Owusu-Manu is an ordained minister of God with dynamic gift of wisdom for the ministry of Jesus Christ. Paapa was born and grew up as a Muslim until his divine paradigm shift to the Kingdom of God. He is a great Bible teacher and God uses him powerfully.

He has been a teacher for over 19 years in both Ghana and abroad (London, United Kingdom). His areas of specialties are Business Enterprise and Entrepreneurship Education, Primary and Adult Numeracy, Internal Verification (Moderation) and Quality Assurance, Teacher Trainer and Inspection Strategist. He has worked and provided consultancy services to over nine inner London HM Prisons/Young Offender Institute as an OLASS Advanced Practitioner for quality improvement, coaching and mentoring. He is currently working as a Lead Internal Quality Assurance in all the inner London Prisons and four Private Training Colleges in London.

Paapa has studied in four reputable Higher Education Universities in London. He is a speaker at Universities on "Teaching in Prison as an Alternative Experience" and has mentored numerous assessors,

THE SECRET OF WEALTH CREATION

BREAKING THE CYCLE OF POVERTY

teachers, lecturers and internal verifiers/moderators in London.
- ✓ He is the founder of Decision Time Centre which deals with:
- ✓ Publication of Children's Educational Materials and resources.
- ✓ Children and Youth Mentoring: Talks & Discussions on reducing offending &
- ✓ re-offending (Decision Time Prison Talk).
- ✓ Offender & Ex-offender Education: Reducing crime, offending and re-offending through biblical principles (Crime to Entrepreneurship).
- ✓ Publication of Christian Literature (Quick Reads) to promote the Gospel of Jesus Christ.
- ✓ Educational Quality Assurance Improvement and Teacher Education.
- ✓ Speaker on Offender Education at Universities, Colleges, Schools and Churches.
- ✓ Business Start Ups, Enterprise and Entrepreneurship Education.

Enquiries & Contact:
info@decisiontime.org.uk
paapa.manu@decisiontime.org.uk
www.decisiontime.org.uk

THE SECRET OF WEALTH CREATION

BREAKING THE CYCLE OF POVERTY

Decision Time Centre

Cover Design: Ben Kobiah Arhin, London

www.ingramcontent.com/pod-product-compliance
Lightning Source LLC
LaVergne TN
LVHW041550070426
835507LV00011B/1021